VICTOR VILLASEÑOR

# Gathering StarDust

ILLUSTRATED BY
JACK WIENS

Waterside Productions
Cardiff, California

First Printing, 2024

ISBN-13: 978-1-962984-45-4 (hardcover)
ISBN-13: 978-1-962984-46-1 (ebook)

Library of Congress Control Number: 2024919322

*Gathering StarDust* is published by: Waterside Productions.

For information about special discounts for bulk purchases, please direct emails to: sales@waterside.com

Illustrations by Jack Wiens
Book design by Teri Rider

Waterside Productions
2055 Oxford Ave., Cardiff, CA 92007
www.waterside.com

Printed in the USA

# DEDICATION

*This book is dedicated to honoring the Eternal Child within each of us, and especially for Beth, Conor, Diego, Clare, my brother Joseph, and to all others who Passed Over at a very young age.*

*For these ENLIGHTENED SOULS Knew to their Core, even as they came Gathering StarDust from across the Heavens, that they'd be returning Home early to Our Other Side of Being in order to help us on This Side.*

*So, none of these Young Ancient Souls, Passed Over before their time. Actually they Passed right on time in Rhythm with the Great Miraculous Symphony of Our Forever ExpandingContracting Universe!*

"I had a Dream. I had a Prayer. I had a Vision. We're All going Somewhere Together."

*Tim Redbird Whitefox*

"Whatever you can do or dream you can do, begin it. Boldness has genius, power, and magic."

*Johann Wolfgang von Goethe*

"I know God will not give me anything I can't handle. I just wish He didn't have so much Trust in me."

*Mother Teresa of Calcutta*

"When a person really desires something, all the universe conspires to help that person realize their dream."

*Paulo Coelho*

"Before civilization you, me, we, all of us were like weeds all over Our Mother Earth. Wild of Heart. Alive of Soul. And Indestructible in Faith as we reach for the SunLight of God!"

*Doña Margarita*

"Every day thousands of geniuses live and die undiscovered—either by themselves or by others."

*Mark Twain*

"It took me a long time not to judge myself through other's eyes."

*Sally Field*

"Out of clutter, find simplicity. From discord, find harmony. In the middle of difficulty lies opportunity."

*Albert Einstein*

"Success is not final, failure is not fatal. It is the courage to continue that counts."

*Winston Churchill*

"Whether you know where you're going or not, you'll get there anyway."

*Henry Miller*

"My idea of heaven is a great big baked potato and someone to share it with."

*Oprah Winfrey*

# CONTENTS

# My True Story

I was born at home on May 11, 1940 in the old *Mexican Barrio* of Carlsbad, California, which we, *la gente*, called *CarlosMalo*.

Back then, Carlsbad was just a tiny village surrounded by fields of produce and cutting flowers and orchards of avocados, oranges, and lemons.

And I was raised up in the Old Yaqui Way by my Native American grandmother with the understanding that we lived in Heaven, here on Mother Earth. For every day is *otro Milagro de Dios*, another Miracle gifted us by God.

Enjoy!

Victor Villaseñor

# Thankfulness

# Who are You?
# Who am I?
# Who are We?

Come, and take my hand, and let us be children once again, and this time be raised up together by my Yaqui Native American grandmother.

Oh, I remember well, every morning my plump old *mamagrande* would bundle me up in her warm *zarape* blanket, and take me across our little back yard, past her big avocado tree, and to her little house in back alongside the alley, and here, every morning the magic began.

"Place your two little hands over your heart, my little love, and sing along with me," she'd say.

Quickly, I'd put my little hands over my heart, so I could sing along with my grandmother.

"Good morning! Good morning! Good morning!" we'd sing together with so much fun and *gusto*.

Then she'd tell me, "Look, Our Father Sun, the Right Eye of God, has just come up over that distant hilltop, shooting rays of beautiful golden light and hope all across the land. And Our Brother Birds are singing, and Our Sister Flowers are turning their happy faces and smiling. Oh, we're all so happy giving thanks together to Our Lord God Creator."

I'd look and it was true. The birds in all the trees around us were singing with their beaks pointed up to the heavens. And the flowers were smiling and dancing with all their beauty. And my grandmother and I couldn't stop smiling we were also so happy giving thanks.

"Oh, *mijito,*" my *mamagrande* would say, "can't you just feel it? Our Mother Earth and us and all the rest of Creation just gets so happy giving thanks first thing every morning to *Papito Dios,* who has once more Blessed us with another wondrous day full of Miraculous Sunlight."

And now, my grandmother would tickle me and kiss me and I'd kick my little legs, screeching with joy, and she'd tell me to watch the leaves of our big tall trees shimmering with the magic lifegiving Sunlight of Our Right Eye of God.

And I'd look and see that it was true. Now the leaves of all the trees were shimmering with such joy that our trees were glowing with a soft golden light.

"And that soft golden light you see glowing all about our trees," my *mamagrande* would say to me, "is the Sacred Magic of Our Lord God's Holy Breath gently touching the Souls of Our Trees.

"You see, my little Love, Our Wonderful Mother Earth and all of Creation is alive and breathing and has a Soul. And the word for God and the word for Breath are the exact same word in my mother language.

"So with every GodBreath, Our Almighty Blesses every morning Sacred Magic Life, *La Vida*, into the Soul of Our Beloved Mother Earth and all Trees, and all Flowers, and all Birds, and Ants, and Flies, and even into all the Rocks, who are now warming up with God's wondrous Love*Amor*, and beginning to purr."

"And us, too!" I'd shout. "Us, too!"

"Yes," she'd say, laughing, "and of course, Our Holy Creator also Blesses every morning Sacred Magic into the Soul of us, Human People."

"Yes," I'd say, reaching out to touch the rocks closest to us, "so we, too, can purr like the rocks and our big old mother cat with her kittens!"

"Exactly, and our purring starts right here, behind your little left ear," she'd say, tickling my ear and it felt so really good. "And that purring goes around the back of our head to our right ear, so we can now know that our Hearts and Souls are full to the brim of Our Almighty's Sacred Magic.

"And all these Wonderful Miracles, you, my little Love*Amor*, helped create when you came across the Universe with your own Guardian Angel, gathering StarDust, so the two of you could help *Papito Dios* plant Heaven on Earth.

"So always remember that this is who we human people are, *mijito*, God's helpers, because Our Almighty can't do it without us. In fact, since Timeless Time we've been doing *Papito Dios'* Holy Sacred Work of planting Heaven on 1,000s and 1,000s of other Mother Earths throughout all Our Universe!"

Hearing this, I'd laugh with *carcajadas*, kicking my little legs with joy. Oh, this was so wonderful! *Papito Dios* couldn't do it without my Guardian Angel and me bringing Him the StarDust that we'd gathered up from all the different Stars.

"So realize, *mijito*," my grandmother would now say, blowing little kisses on my bellybutton, "this is why you and every child are so very special, and need to be so very, very careful with what it is you plant. Do you plant anger and yelling, or . . . do you plant kindness and lots of hugging and Love*Amor*?"

"We plant lots of hugging and Love*Amor*!" I'd shout.

"And why?"

"Because it's more fun!"

"Exactly," she'd say, "and so now hug me and let's rub noses together, because with our ears and our noses, it's so easy to fill ourselves all up with God's good feeling Holy Magic."

And it was true. Next to having my ears tickled and rubbing my tiny nose against my grandmother's big round warm nose, the greatest was to know that we were full to the brim of God's Holy Magic.

Then laughing with *gusto*, she'd say, "For always remember that we, human people, aren't as strong as the ants, and we're not as quick as the flies, and we're not as smart as the bees, and we don't have thick fur to keep us warm like the fox, and we don't have wings like the mighty eagle, and so this is why we hug and laugh so much, and then every night, when we go to sleep, we travel with Our Guardian Angel back up to Heaven to sleep in *Papito Dios'* warm loving arms.

“Sleeping with Our Almighty is what we human people do best, *mijito*. And this is why you and your Guardian Angel love to sleep and take little naps, because you awake smiling and sometimes even laughing.”

And my grandmother was right. My Guardian Angel and I would always awake smiling and sometimes even laughing with *carcajadas*, feeling so wonderful to know that were were forever connected to Our Holy Creator with our purring that began behind our left ear and traveled around the back of our head to our right ear.

Standing up and stretching, my *mamagrande* would now say, “Okay, *mis huaraches*, it’s time for us to go to work. We’ve done Our First Two Miracles of the day.

“First, we’ve awoke, and we’ve filled up our Hearts and Souls with God’s Love*Amor* with our every Breath.

“Second, we’ve given thanks along with Our Sister Flowers and Our Brother Birds to the Right Eye of Our Holy Creator, so now it’s time for us to make use of our wonderful God-given hands and go to work, just like the birds who’ve stopped singing and flown off to the fields in search of food.”

And so my *mamagrande* and I would now go over to our little garden next to our leaky old faucet with the broken handle.

All night the leaky faucet had been filling up my grandmother's great big *olla*, and now she, with her big pan and me with my little cup would scoop up water and walk across to the circle garden of Our Three Sacred Sisters: corn, string beans and squash.

First, we'd planted our corn, giving it a head start to grow tall and straight and strong. Then we'd planted our string beans so they could wind their way up the cornstalk. And now last, we planted our squash so that their big leaves would give shade to our little circular garden, so then we'd only have to use a little bit of water to raise up our whole garden.

Oh, I'd love walking with my little cup back and forth from our old leaky faucet to our garden, spilling water on my legs and feet. And soon my pathway was all muddy, and the sandy soil felt so good between my tiny toes.

And then when I'd slip and fall down, I'd always wiggle my naked little butt in the sandy wet soil just like ducks do in a pond, and oh, this would feel so itchy good and wonderful!

This was also just about the same time when my mother would come out the back door of our family's home and call out to us that breakfast was ready. *Chorizo* with *huevos* and freshly homemade *tortillas*.

I'd screech with joy, I was so hungry after having given thanks to God and then done so much good-feeling hard work!

MI CASA ES TU CASA

# Adventure

After breakfast, I'd get so excited, I could pop! Our Father Sun was now four fists off the horizon, and my *mamagrande* would put me in our little red wagon along with the vegetables we'd picked.

It wasn't very hot yet, so this was a good time for us to go around the *Barrio* trading our vegetables for tomatoes and eggs and goat cheese, and then best of all, for hot freshly baked Mexican sweet breads, which were, of course, my favorites.

Our Mexican *Barrio de CarlosMalo* lay just south of the main part of Carlsbad, California, and our streets weren't paved and didn't have sidewalks like the Anglo part of town.

Our streets were dirt and had great big potholes, and our goats and pigs ran free along with all our cats and dogs.

It was our vegetable and flower gardens that we fenced in, which made a lot of sense, since flowers and vegetables couldn't run around all over the place searching for food like our goats and pigs, dogs and cats, and of course, our chickens.

"Now remember, *mijito*," my *mamagrande* would tell me when we were ready to go, "all human people are really good of heart, so this is why every time we leave our home, it is Our Blessed Duty to say something or do something to make at least 10 people open up their hearts, and smile and laugh.

"This, *mijito*, is how we, Ordinary People, can help *Papito Dios* bring out the best in human people, and also help make this a kinder, better world.

"Okay, my little Love*Amor*, are you ready? Here we go, you and me and Our Guardian Angels with our fresh vegetables that we raised up with lots and lots of Love*Amor* and, of course, with *Papito Dios*'s Blessings."

And saying this, she'd start pushing our little wooden homemade red wagon with me and our baskets full of vegetables. First, we'd go out into our side street, then we'd turn right and go along the side of my father's pool hall with all the boxes of smelly empty beer bottles.

Sal's
POOL
HALL
BEER
BEER
BEER

Then at the corner, we'd turn right again and now, oh, wow, we were on the main street of our big exciting *Barrio de CarlosMalo*!

Why, the whole place was alive with big kids shouting and chasing balls, and dogs running and barking, and some big old mud-covered trucks with huge tires and roaring motors.

Then suddenly, one big truck slammed on its breaks and started honking. And right there alongside the truck's big front tires was a brown and white mother pig with her bunch of squealing little cute baby pigs crossing the street, and she was in no big hurry.

After all, this was her street, too, and it had so many deep potholes that all of the trucks and cars had to drive real slow, especially after a good rain when the biggest potholes would fill up with water and the kids of the *Barrio* would play in them like they were swimming pools.

Finally, the truck driver, who was a stranger and didn't know the way of our *Barrio de CarlosMalo*, quit honking and he, too, just smiled as he watched the mother pig and her little ones cross the street.

And it was a very good thing that this truck driver did this, because *Doña Cuca*, the proud owner of the pigs, was already half-way across the street with her big broom and ready to clubber the stranger in the face through his open window if he'd kept honking.

But seeing him now smiling at her mother pig, *Doña Cuca* lowered her broom, and when the truck driver turned and saw the colorfully dressed old woman with her big broom in hand, he started laughing with *carcajadas*.

"Were you really going to hit me with that broom?" he asked.

"You damn right!" shouted *Doña Cuca* loud enough for all the people watching to hear her. "So just thank your lucky stars that your mother raised you to respect mothers! Because one more honk at my mother pig caring for her little ones, and you would have gotten a broom slashing in the face you would remember for the rest of your life!"

And all the people of the *Barrio* who were watching started laughing and applauding. *Mamagrande* and I, too, laughed and applauded.

Then my grandmother continued pushing me down the busy street of our wonderful wild *Barrio*, and up ahead, we made our first stop at the home of my *mamagrande's* best friend.

Her name was *Doña Gloria*, and just like my grandmother's house – that my dad had built for 25 dollars – her house was also ten feet by fifteen feet. And in this tiny space, *Gloria* had her kitchen, her bedroom, her living room, and her corner alter where she did her praying and embroidering, just like my *mamagrande*.

But very different than my grandmother's house, which was painted all white, *Doña Gloria's* home was painted bright pink with turquoise trim around the window and front door.

Pink, I was told, brought in our good happy feelings of Life, *la Vida*, and turquoise brought in our healing Sacred Spirits, so this was why my *mamagrande* had also painted turquoise around her windows and door of her all-white house.

Then we'd no more than stopped, when my grandmother and her best friend began their juicy happy ritual of smiling and laughing and hugging, then making the sign of the cross over themselves and giving thanks together for God having once more Blessed us with another glorious day of Gold Raining Miracles.

"Did you see the sunrise this morning?" asked *Gloria*, who was also colorfully dressed just like *Doña Cuca*.

"But of course," said my *mamagrande,* who was very simply dressed in brown and white.

"Oh, I swear that this morning Our Right Eye of God winked at me," said *Gloria*, giggling.

"I'm sure He did," said my grandmother, laughing with *carcajadas*. "For I swear, every year, *mujer,* us old ones get more beautiful, and ya, ya, ya!"

*Gloria* screeched. "Oh, you really know how to make an old woman feel wonderful!"

"Old are the mountains," said my *mamagrande*, still laughing, "for the beauty of good-hearted women is ageless!"

"You're absolutely right," said *Gloria*, "aging for us grandmothers is like rivers cutting deep beautiful wrinkled canyons into Our Mother Earth!"

And so my grandmother and her best friend continued talking and laughing and giving each other compliments, but I quit paying attention.

Because what *Doña Gloria* was really famous for wasn't just having the finest chickens in the *Barrio*, but she was also the proud owner of our famous big red rooster who, legend had it, was the king of our whole *Barrio*.

Oh, this red rooster king story I'd heard at least 100 times. And what happened was that one day a great big mean dog from the other side of town had come into our *Barrio* attacking our goats and pigs and little dogs, and then he'd cornered a mother chicken with baby chicks under the big knotted elephant foot of one of our huge eucalyptus trees.

And this was when *Doña Gloria's* big fighting red rooster came screeching to the rescue. People who saw it, say he leaped ten feet into the air and came flying down with his huge gigantic wings flared out screaming like the devil himself.

Instantly the big mean dog crouched down in terror and let out a howl of pain and turned tail. But our big red rooster didn't let up, and he continued riding and spurring the big dog all the way out of our *Barrio*.

Then it was said that once our King Kong rooster vanquished the great big mean dog, he came strutting back down the street of our *Barrio* with such kingly elegance that *Gloria's* eggs instantly doubled in price, going from 2 cents an egg to 4 cents.

For now all the men of our *Barrio* only wanted to eat eggs from chickens that were bred by the king of our *Barrio,* so that they, too, would then always be fearless in defending their *familias*.

Oh, I loved it! It was so exciting to be living in a neighborhood so full of juicy gossip, and great legends.

I must've fallen asleep, because after trading our vegetables for goat milk, then for flowers for my mother, I don't remember the last few stops my *mamagrande* made.

All I knew was that she was now huffing and puffing and breathing real hard as she pushed our little red wagon. So I knew this meant she'd taken another right turn, and we were now where the ground got soft and sandy and she had to push harder.

And also, this was the Magic Place where every day, I'd see 1,000s of Angels shimmering in the branches of a long line of huge eucalyptus tree. Oh, it was always so cool and shady and quiet here, far away from all the busyness of our *Barrio*. And my grandmother would now open up her blouse and wipe her face and neck with her white handkerchief with the little embroidered green leaves and tiny red flowers.

Heaven, my *mamagrande* would always tell me, was peacefully embroidering with our God-given hands.

Heaven was also quietly praying with our rosary in hand, fingering the smooth little beads.

And Heaven was also when we stopped here every day to take a little rest together, and quietly look up into these magnificent huge tall trees and see their branches full of dancing Angels.

"You see, *mijito*," she'd explain to me, "Heaven is with us all day long when we start out our day by giving thanks to Our Holy Creator's Blessed Right Eye. For then, my little love, we human people see Life, *la Vida*, through Our Lord God's Right Eye, too.

"Oh, *mijito*, just look up into this great old tree's branches, and through Our Almighty's Right Eye, we not only see dancing Angels, we also see Beauty in all her old broken places.

"For in Our Hearts, we can feel to Our Bones all the storms and strikes of lightning this magnificent old tree has endured."

And I'd look, and it was true. Not only did I see dancing Angels, but I could also see and feel the pain of her old torn places.

But then I could also see that at these old broken places there was a Golden Glowing Light and rich new green growth.

"Oh, what a joy it is," my *mamagrande* would now say with tears coming to her eyes, "to see all of life, oh, so beautiful when our human people eyes see through Our Almighty's Right Eye."

Seeing tears now running down my grandmother's face, I'd quickly scrambled out of our little wagon and go to my *mamagrande*, cuddling up with her on the huge knotted-up elephant foot of her gigantic eucalyptus tree.

And she'd hold me close and tears would now come to my eyes, too, and she'd use her embroidered white handkerchief to wipe my eyes.

"And always remember, *mijito*, that our tears aren't sad tears. No, these are happy tears. For God has Blessed me to live long enough to pass on to you the Sacred Knowledge of Our Original Instructions, and you are young enough to receive them.

"You see, all Living Life has their own Original Instructions. That's why bees know what to do, the flies know what to do, the ants, the frogs, the chickens, and especially the butterflies.

"And the First Instruction for us human people is to always remember that *Papito Dios* is Forever and Ever Breathing Love*Amor* into All of Creation."

Hearing this, I'd get so excited that I'd kick my little legs, shouting "Yes, and with our every Breath we are forever filling up our Hearts with *Papito Dios'* Love*Amor*!"

"Exactly, and this is why we each need to have our very own quiet place to go to every day, so we can cry our happy tears.

"For these quiet gentle tears of ours, without anger or malice, open up our Hearts and allow our Souls to Breathe."

"Breathe in *Papito Dios' Amor*!" I quickly added.

"Yes," she said, smiling, "for how else could we human people have survived for all these 1,000s of 1,000s of years since –"

"Since we aren't as smart as the bees," I said. "And we aren't as strong as the ants, and we have no fur like the fox, if –"

“If it wasn’t for us singing good morning,” my *mamagrande* began saying along with me “to the Right Eye of God, so that then we have Heaven about us all day long!”

Then just like magic we’d have butterflies come to us. Two or three at first, then whole swarms. And my grandmother and I would put our hands out, and the butterflies would land on them.

Oh, I felt so Blessed and full of *Papito Dios'* Magic Love*Amor*. And my *mamagrande* would now sing to me in her Native Yaqui Language with a lot of tongue clicks, and each word sounded like Heaven.

Then laughing with joy, she'd get up off the elephant foot of her favorite eucalyptus tree, and she'd put me back in our little homemade red wagon.

"Okay, *mis huaraches*!" she'd now say, standing up tall, and my Yaqui grandmother was tall. In fact, she was taller than almost all of the other women of our *Barrio*.

"We've done it! We're finished! We traded all our vegetables, and we've said something or done something to make at least 10 human people smile and laugh, helping *Papito Dios* make this a kinder, better world.

"So, well, we can now head for home with the *gran gusto* of having Our Almighty's Love*Amor* Purring going on back and forth from ear to ear around the back of our head!"

And saying this, my plump old *mamagrande* began dancing and laughing as she now pushed our little red wagon and me past the last gigantic eucalyptus trees, and turned right into the little alley taking us home.

And I, too, was now laughing and waving my arms with joy as we'd go down our rocky dirt alley between the large backyards of our *Barrio*.

Bright bedsheets of orange and yellow and red and white were hanging on the tall drying lines and swaying with the breeze.

Women and children were cutting with big knives and long-handled brooms the large juicy red and orange and yellow prickly pears off their tall green cactus plants.

Others were working in their vegetable gardens, and they now all turned laughing and waving as my dancing laughing *mamagrande* and I came down the alley.

Oh, it was such a joy to come home every day knowing that we'd helped *Papito Dios* make Our *Barrio de CarlosMalo* a place of Big Big Happy Magic Love*Amor*!

# Dreams

Getting home, my grandmother and I would put almost everything we'd traded for in my mother's refrigerator up at our bigger house in front. Then we'd start making balls of goat milk soap.

Goat milk soap with added herbs, my *mamagrande* would explain to me, was the Miracle why she had soft skin and no wrinkles on her face and hands.

In fact, goat milk soap with added herbs was the reason why my dad and mother were so happy, and even old couples still loved the *¡ay, ay, ay!*

Then after we'd finished making the goat milk soap balls, my mother would sometimes bathe me with one of our freshly made soap balls, and oh, it would feel like Heaven it was so smooth and good feeling.

And now I'd get to lay down and take a nap with my mother before my older sister and brother came home from school.

But other times, it was my *mamagrande* who'd bathe me, and I'd lay down and take a nap with her. And either way, this was another Heaven for me sleeping all bundled up close with my mother or with my grandmother.

Then when I'd awake, it was another fantastic, wonderful Heaven!

It was now dinner time, and the whole house smelled so good with all the cooking, and ours was always a loud happy family dinner with our father sitting at the head of the table.

And every evening our dad would get in trouble telling us funny true stories about the Mexican Revolution and growing up in *Los Altos de Jalisco, México* with wild herds of cattle and horses and goats and pigs.

And he'd also tell us that back then every ranch had a pack of ten to fifteen dogs that were so ferocious that even the wolves and

mountain lions didn't come near their *rancho grandes*.

Oh, we all loved our father's stories, especially when he would tell us how the leader of their pack of dogs was an ugly little old mother dog.

"Oh, she was as mean and ugly and bossy as our good neighbor *Doña Cuca*, who paints her face like a clown and wears such colorful clothes, that she thinks she's gorgeous!"

"Salvador!" our mother Lupe would yell at our father. "Don't talk like that! You're teaching our kids to be disrespectful!"

"Good! Too much respect and we would have no life to live with all laws of our Church, and the laws of the land, and especially all the opinions of our people who say, 'don't do that,' and 'don't do this!'

"Oh, I hate the rich! I hate the rich!" our father would now begin to sing with *carcajadas*. "The rich are no good! No good! No good!"

"Stop it, Salvador!"

"But why? My little old bag of Indian bones mother would always say, if we talk bad about anyone, God will punish us and make us just like them!

"So come on, God, punish me! Punish me good, and make me rich! So I can buy a big ranch here in *CarlosMalo* like we used to have in *Los Altos de Jalisco*!

"Come on, *amor de me vida*, let's make a kiss!" he said, getting up and coming around the table to our mother. "You and your *familia,* who suffered so much, know that we got to wake up God with a good poke of fun in the ribs or we get *nada, nada*, nothing!"

Then raising up his arms and looking skyward, our dad shouted, "So come on, God, punish me! Punish me! Punish me, and make my whole *familia* BIG BIG RICH!"

By now our mother would finally give up and allow our dad to kiss her. For there was no stopping our father once he started laughing and singing and wanting to kiss our mother.

And kiss they did. A big, long kiss. And us kids, who'd been laughing, but also scared that God Almighty might come down from Heaven and really do our father in, were now relieved and happy.

Then after dinner our dad would light up a big cigar, put on his *vaquero*-cowboy hat, and go to work at his pool hall.

And all the rest of us would get up and help our mother and grandmother to clean up the kitchen and put everything away, and we'd still be smiling and laughing.

Our Father Sun was going down and once more I was so excited, I could pop. Because now, every evening, my *mamagrande* would once again bundle me up in her colorful *zarape* blanket and quickly take me across our little backyard to her big old rocking chair that was by her outhouse alongside her big avocado tree.

And because her outhouse was alongside her avocado tree, my *mamagrande's* avocados were the biggest and creamiest avocados in all our *Barrio*.

"Look, *mijito*," my grandmother would say to me, once we'd cuddled up together in her big old

rocking chair, "see how Our Father Sun, the Right Eye of God, finishes up His Holy Work every evening by painting us a beautiful sky."

I'd look and it was true. Beyond our tall trees the whole sky looked like Heaven with colors of orange and red and gold and silver streaks of light coming down through the pinky-rose clouds.

"Oh, my little love, how Blessed are we who see Life, *la Vida*, through the Right Eye of Our Holy Creator."

And saying this, she'd kiss me and kiss me, then say, "Okay, so now let us place our hands over our Heart*Corazones* and say, "Good night, Father Sun, good night, and have a good rest. For now Our Mother Moon, the Left Eye of God, will start gifting us a Miraculous Night full of Dreams and Magic.

"For this is who we human people are when every night we go back up to Heaven along with our Guardian Angel and sleep in Your Warm Loving Arms.

"We are Your Dream Makers of Magic and Miracles. We are Your Holy Instruments in helping You, Our Mother Moon, to plant Heaven on Mother Earths throughout Our Whole Entire Universe!"

"And all these Stars are our *familia*," I quickly added.

"Yes, *mijito*, all these Stars, who are now coming out and winking at us, are Our *Familia* who came down here to Mother Earth, and planted their StarDust Holy Gardens, then returned to the Heavens from where we all come."

"Uncle!" I yelled. "Our Uncle *Grande*!"

"Yes," said my *mamagrande* laughing, "and that biggest brightest Star of all that we see up in the Heavens is Our Great Great Great Great Uncle *Don Pedo*, Mr. Farts, who was so full of joy and gas when he was down here on Mother Earth, that we can see that he's still full of exploding gas and joy up in the Heavens!"

"Yes!" I yelled, laughing with such *carcajadas*, that I, too, now let go of a stream of little farts.

"Yes, you, too. For who knows, you enjoy your *peditos* so much that you might end up being one of the biggest brightest Stars in all the Heavens!"

And I'd laugh and laugh and she'd rub my little belly and sing, *"Sana, sana, colita de rana, hechate un pedito y sanate mañana!"* Get well, get well, little tail of a polywog, give a little fart and be well tomorrow!

And just then, a whole *familia* of coyotes joined us, howling and yapping along with our singing and laughing.

Papa coyotes. Mother coyotes. And little high-pitched baby coyotes. All of us serenading Our Mother Moon, the Left Eye of God, and the great vastness of Our Welcoming *Familia* of Sparkling Bright Stars.

Then a great big owl came in to land in the avocado tree right next to us, and she began hooting, and her eyes were huge and round and bright. Oh, it was all getting so Magical.

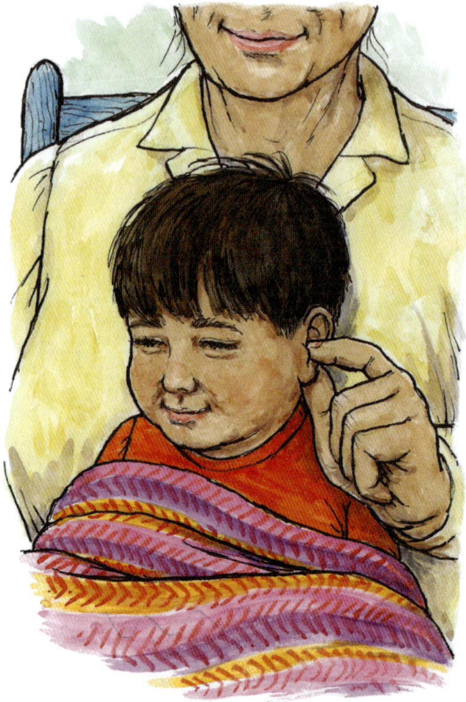

"Okay, now let's check your little ears," said my grandmother, taking hold of my left ear, "so you will feel the Purring of *Papito Dios* all night long."

Oh, I loved this! The way my *mamagrande* would now gently take hold of my left ear with her thumb behind the lobe of my ear and her index finger inside my ear.

"This ear is a little tight tonight," she said, "so I'm going to have to loosen it a little by turning it and twisting it, then giving it a nice little massage."

And oh, it felt so good, especially with her finger inside my ear going around and around as her thumb turned and twisted my ear lobe, then gave little massaging tugs.

“So how does your ear now feel?” she’d asked.

“Like Heaven!”

“Exactly,” she’d say. “Because that’s what we’re doing, starting with your left ear, on the HeartSide of your body, preparing you for your journey up to Heaven along with your Guardian Angel, so you two can sleep together, all cuddling up in Her Almighty’s warm loving arms.

“Yes, cuddling!” I’d say, loving what she’d done to my left ear. “So now do my other ear,” I’d add with excitement.

“Yes, of course,” she’d say, “now let’s check your right ear. Our EarthSide of your body. Oh, this one is a little loose, so we’ll have to tighten it.”

And saying this, she’d massage my right ear with her index finger inside and her thumb behind my ear lobe, and this got to feeling so good that now my whole body began tingling with wonderful feelings.

"There," she'd now say, "both ears are balanced. So can you feel –"

"Yes!" I'd say, excitedly. "I can now feel *Mamá Dios'* Purring from ear to ear and tickling the whole back of my head!"

"Good. Excellent. And now close your HeadEyes, my little love, and open your HeartEyes, so you and your Guardian Angel can start your Soul Travel.

"For remember, sleeping with Our Almighty is what we human people do best. And this is why you and your Guardian Angel love to sleep and take little naps, because you wake up smiling and sometimes even laughing.

"And also remember that as you two travel back across the Heavens, you'll pass many of the Stars from which you two gathered StarDust. And you might see little Glowing Specks of StarDust that you wish you'd originally brought with you.

"But don't stop. Keep going. And after you've slept all night in Our Holy Creator's warm loving arms, you'll know if you and your Guardian Angel want to gather up those Glowing Golden Specs of StarDust on your way back.

"For this is Our Infinite Rain of Gold that we human people have been bringing to all Our Holy Gardens – along with Our Star Cousins from Our Six Sister Mother Planets – ever since Our Mother Earth was young and Our Star *Familia* spoke and we human people knew how to listen."

But my grandmother's words were now no more than a far, far away Dream. For my Guardian Angel and I were now gone, gone, gone. No longer part of Our Present Mother Earth, and instead in Harmony with Our Big Drum HeartBeat of Our Whole Entire Universe!

One Verse.

One Song.

One United Symphony.

A Dream of Magic.

A Dream of Purring.

A Dream of Warm Love*Amor* Cuddling with Our Holy Almighty Creator Forever and Ever!

We were going Home, recrossing Our Heaven and passing by the Stars from which we'd gathered Our StarDust in order to help *MamáPapá Dios* plant Our Heaven on Mother Earth.

As we human people had been doing on 1,000s and 1,000s of other Mother Earths. For this was who we really are, God's Miracle Makers. God's Helpers in Creating Creation.

"Goodnight, Mother Moon! Goodnight Smiling Mother Moon! Goodnight! Oh, we love You so!"

And hearing us Our Mother Moon danced and got even brighter and happier as my Guardian Angel and I flew past Her.

Oh, we were so happy! BIG BIG HAPPY that we couldn't stop smiling. Oh, being with my plump old *mamagrande* had been Pure Magic all day long, and now it was Pure Magic all night long.

So I took in a great big GodBreath as my Guardian Angel and I continued zooming across Heaven and our little tiny Mother Earth was now no larger than a grain of sand on the Sea Shore of Creation.

And my Guardian Angel and I, on the other hand, were gigantic Soul Instruments stretching out to the furthest reaches of Our Universe!

# Heaven

It was the week before Christmas, and tonight our *Barrio* would start doing their yearly event of *las posadas* for seven consecutive nights.

*Las posadas* is a Latin American reenactment of Mary and Joseph going from door to door with their *burrito*, trying to find a place to spend the night.

And like always in our *Barrio*, local teenagers would play the parts of Mary and Joseph, knocking from door to door, only to end up at *Muñoz's* garage which had once more been converted into a barn and manger.

Oh, this was a huge yearly event with *gente*-people coming in from all north county, including many non-*Latinos* to afterwards enjoy the *tamales, atole, champurrado*, and *piñatas* for the little kids.

And so this evening, seven days before Christmas, we were sitting at the dinner table preparing to just have a small bite to eat when our dad came bursting in through the front door, yelling:

“God is still punishing us BIG TIME! I’ve found our ranch! Our Big Ranch in South Oceanside, and it’s for sale!

“Oh, it’s so beautiful with big orchards of avocados and oranges and lemons, and herds of cattle and horses. And also a huge barn full of modern farm equipment, and even a big brand new red tractor!

"Come on, let's all get in the car and go look at it before it gets dark. It's in South Oceanside, just a couple of miles north of us!"

"Salvador, dinner is ready," said our mother, "and you know that tonight is our first night of our *posadas*. We can go see the ranch tomorrow."

"If we go right now, we'll get back in plenty of time to see our *posadas*."

"Oh, Salvador!" said our mother in frustration. "What makes you even think we can afford a ranch! The truth is that we're just getting by, especially with all the added work of our new liquor store!"

Prohibition was over, and our dad and mom had sold their pool hall, bought a liquor license, and opened the first liquor store in Carlsbad, just one block north of our *Barrio* where the streets were paved.

State liquor licenses were terribly expensive, and our mother hadn't wanted to buy one. But our dad had kept insisting that selling legal liquor was going to be a gold mine, even better than having been a bootlegger.

But there had been tons of documents that needed to be read and signed and our dad didn't know how to read, so our mom had done all the work and the license was finally gotten in her name, too.

And our dad, with a prison record, couldn't legally have anything to do with their liquor store so now it was our mom – and not our dad – who worked long hours day and night, doing merchandise ordering, bookkeeping, payroll, banking, and paying something called taxes that our father hated.

"Lupe! Lupe! We're rich! Just let go of the past, and open your eyes and see where we now are, *mi amor*."

"Yes, I see I'm working! Working like a slave! Oh, Salvador, can't you see that you're just talking foolishness. Even our own people are now leaving California and going back to Mexico, where they can feel safe."

Pearl Harbor had only happened a couple of years ago, so people were terrified Japan was now any day going to bomb California, too.

"*Mi amor*," said our father, "just calm down, and remember what my little bag of Indian bones *madre* always said, where there's fear, there's opportunity, if we don't got the fear.

"And this is an opportunity of a lifetime. The only reason this beautiful ranch is for sale is because the Canadians, who own it, got scared and ran back to Canada, telling our local judge Cottingham to sell it for whatever he can get.

"And the judge has a lot of people looking, but he hasn't yet been able to close a deal. So this is our chance! Right now!

“Come on! Get in the car and see great big oranges in the middle of winter hanging down from the trees. And avocado trees and lemon trees full of fruit.

“Oh, I tell you, *mi amor*, this is bigger and better than any dream I’ve EVER DREAMED! The horses and cattle are fat from grazing on all the rolling grass hills, that go down all the way to the marsh lands by the sea.”

Tears were streaming down our dad's face. "Lupe, I know how hard you're working and don't have much time for our kids anymore, but please understand, this is a time to rejoice, and give thanks to God after all our years of suffering, that He's now at long last Gifting us Our Dreams!

"Come, give me your hand, *mi amor*," he added with tears still streaming, "and let us accept this gift of our long-awaited Dreams!"

But our mother was still pretty hesitant, until our *mamagrande* spoke.

"*Mijita*, go with him and take the children. I'll keep dinner for when you come back.

"For remember what I've always told you, men don't carry the baby, don't nurse the baby, and so we, women, need to help them to carry and nurse their dreams or they get lost.

"And *mijita*, Salvador's Dream is for the good of your whole *familia*. He's not like so many men, who just think of themselves. So go, Lupita, go and rejoice and take the children," she said, winking at our mother.

Seeing her mother's wink, our mother now finally smiled that crooked little smile of hers full of mischief, and took our dad's hand.

And, of course, our dad's whole face lit up with a huge smile and he drew her close, giving our mother a big, long kiss.

Then we were all up and running out the front door and piling into our dad's big dark green Hudson. And once more our dad began bragging how he had the smartest, wisest mother-in-law in all the world, who, of course, reminded him of his own smart, wise, cunning *madre*.

HUDSON

And it was a quick little drive out of the *Barrio* and through the main part of downtown Carlsbad with paved streets and sidewalks.

Then we got on California State Highway 101, crossed a lagoon with people fishing off a little bridge, and we were now in Oceanside.

Then up ahead we turned right on a dirt road, going past farmhouses with orchards, and a few had corrals, too.

"We're almost there," said our dad, beaming with joy. "And all these are little ranches of ten, twenty, and forty acres. Ours is the last 160-acre ranch. A square mile, stolen, of course, from our local Native Brothers.

"Oh, the Canadians loved this ranch, putting in new orchards and rebuilding old barns and corrals, then even putting in a concrete floor for milking their cows in a clean modern way.

"But the poor people lost their faith in their God-Gifted Dream, and ran! But we *Mexicanos* never run from Life, *la Vida*, and our God-Gifted Dreams no matter what!

"Starving and canons exploding all around us, my little old mother had us kneel down and pray, asking for *María, la Madre de Jesús*, to help us live just one more Holy Moment, then one more Holy Blessed Moment.

“Okay,” he said, now turning left, “from here on, everything is ours on both sides of the road for as far as you can see!

“Look, giant avocado trees on the left, and on the right, orange trees and lemon trees stretching across the flat and up the slope to our grass hills for our cattle and horses!

“Oh, Lupe, *mi amor*, “he said with tears coming to his eyes once again, “I remember how my little bag of Indian bones *madre* always told us how God Loves to Gift Our Dreams to us, especially when we poke Him in the ribs with fun and –”

“Look, a peacock!” shouted our mother excitedly. “He’s so beautiful!”

In the orange trees to the right of us, a tall elegant male peacock was fanning out his enormous arch of colorful tail feathers in courtship with a group of female peacocks.

And the big bright oranges hanging in the trees all about the flock of brightly-colored birds looked so Beautiful, so Magical that it, simply, took our Breath away.

"Yes, and those peacocks are ours, too. They're the watchdogs of our ranch. I've been told that even the coyotes are cautious of hunting our pheasants here, because of the screeching scream of our half-wild peacocks."

"Oh, Salvador," said our mother now reaching out and taking our father's hand, "this ranch is a Dream come true. Ever since a child I've dreamed of one day having peacocks."

"Yes, I know," he said, taking her hand and caressing it, then kissing it.

And our mother drew close to our dad, hugging him, but I wasn't paying much attention to our parents anymore.

On both sides of the road were gigantic towering eucalyptus trees way taller than the orchards of avocados and lemons and oranges. And their huge limbs came together over the top of us.

Oh, Miracle of Miracles, it was like we'd entered a tall Magic Tunnel of gigantic trees with elephant feet and their limbs full of Dancing Angels above us and all around us.

I don't remember too much more after that about our first visit to our *rancho grande*, except when we finally got to the house where we would be living.

The house was big and old and had a huge happy fat pepper tree in front. But, oh, once we went inside and I had to go to the bathroom, it was love at first sight!

Everyone was talking and our dad was explaining that yes, he knew this house was old. In fact, over 100 years old and falling apart.

And, yes, the Canadians had put all their money into the barns, and corrals, and farm equipment, and even into the bunk house for their ranch hands.

"But don't worry," he was saying. "In time, we can tear this one down and just build us a new house."

Hearing this, I almost screamed. Because I didn't want this old house to ever be torn down.

Why, in the corner of the bathroom behind the toilet, the two walls had separated up by the ceiling, and beautiful green vines with yellow flowers were now growing on the inside walls and almost all the way down to the toilet.

Oh, this was as beautiful as my *mamagrande's* old outhouse with her little corner altar and potted flowers and the long beams of *Papito Dios*' soft Golden Sunlight coming in through the cracks between the boarded walls.

Driving back to our *Barrio de CarlosMalo*, our dad told us kids not to say one word about our *rancho grande* to anyone. That we had to keep it a secret until we'd closed our deal with Judge Cottingham.

I don't remember too much about our *posadas* that year. All I knew was I was waiting for me and my grandmother to be alone so I could tell her about the fantastic things I'd seen at our ranch.

"Oh, *mamagrande*," I said to her excitedly once we were alone and she was putting me to bed, "as we drove into our ranch, there's a great big tall long Magic Tunnel of gigantic elephant trees.

"And these trees are so old and happy that the toes of their elephant feet are wiggling, and the Dancing Angels on their big, long limbs are singing along with the sound of the sea."

"Yes, I know."

"You know?"

"Of course, through *Papito Dios's* Right Eye I was with you, *mijito*."

"You were with me?"

"I was with all of you," she said, kissing me, "and I'll always be with all of you, even long after I leave my earthly body and return to Spirit."

"Then you also saw the green vines and yellow flowers in the –"

"In the corner above the toilet in the bathroom, yes, of course. Your whole Heart*Corazón* was open with joy, giving Life, *la Vida*, to your *Alma*Soul, so then, of course, I was with you."

I was speechless.

"And now tell me," she said, "what else did you see in that corner up by the ceiling above the toilet?"

I shrugged. I couldn't think of anything else.

"Just close your HeadEyes, my little *mijito* Love*Amor* and open your HeartEyes, and take in a few great big deep GodBreaths, and you'll see Magic."

Suddenly, I saw it. "There's a little tiny bird's nest with red string woven into it!"

"Yes, a hummingbird's nest, who will be coming back in the spring. And your HeadEyes saw this, but it takes Our HeartEyes to register it.

"And that's why you wanted to scream when your father said something about tearing the old house down."

"So then, *mamagrande*, you also knew what I was feeling, and even thinking?"

"Didn't Our Lord Jesus tell us that we each have the Kingdom of God within us?"

I nodded. This I'd heard many times at St. Patrick's Catholic Church on Sundays.

"Well, we do. And Our Holy Creator's Kingdom includes all there is, so when we see life through His Right Eye, then we also know all there is to know.

"So, my little love, have no fear of that old house being torn down. Your father was raised in Our Old Native Way by his mother, *Doña Margarita*, as a woman for the first seven years of his life, so he is a man balanced in Our Holy Magic of Our Father Sun and of Our Mother Moon.

"In fact, that's why he told you – just as you were turning into your *rancho grande* – that we *los Mezclados* don't lose faith and run even when we're starving and canons are exploding all around us.

"For like he said, always remember that this is Our Time to Pray, asking Our Sacred *Madre de Dios* to Bless us with just one more Holy Moment of Life, *la Vida*, then another Blessed Moment.

"And in Our Spirit World One Holy Moment is, of course, an Eternity," she said, smiling, and a soft Glowing Golden Light now came in all about her.

"So, then, you weren't just seeing us through the Right Eye of God. You were actually living with us within *Papito Dios*."

"With my every Breath," she said, smiling, and her Glowing Light grew Brighter and Brighter.

“Oh, *mamagrande*, “I now said, “you’re now all Aglow just like we see Our Trees do every morning when we’re Giving Thanks.”

“Yes, I know,” she said.

“Will I ever glow, too?” I asked.

She laughed. “My little love, you are Aglow.”

"I am?"

"Yes, and so are many other human people also Aglow, but they just can't see it, because they were never given their Original Instructions."

"And I will see them glowing even when they can't see themselves glowing?" I asked.

"Oh, yes, my little love, and they will look so very beautiful to you, even when they can't see their own Miraculous Beauty.

"This is why it's Our Blessed Duty every time we leave our home to say something or do something to make at least 10 people smile and laugh.

"You see, part of Our Original Instructions is to help *Papito Dios* make this a kinder, better world just as we've been doing throughout the Universe since ever."

I suddenly felt a little bit scared. What if I failed? And she saw my worried look and laughed.

"But it's not for us to worry," she said. "For we're all full to the brim with Our Almighty's Magic, so Our Holy Magic can't be stopped no matter what.

"Look, your father was also right when he referred to those Canadians as poor people who'd lost their Faith in their God-Gifted Dream, and ran.

"For to run away from a God-Gifted Dream locks up Our Heart*Corazones* tighter than we can possibly ever imagine, and all but destroys our *Alma*Soul.

"So that's why all your life, *mijito*, you go, you go, you go for your Dreams with all your God-Gifted Magic Powers!

"Oh, I tell you these poor hard-working, good-hearted Canadians are now living up in the cold north in agony with freezing hands, that were warm good-feeling hands down here when they milked their cows in their modern clean warm milking barn."

I smiled.

Oh, I felt so Blessed.

# Fulfillment

Our dad had done it!

With cash in hand, he'd gone to Judge Cottingham, and man to man, he'd made a fantastic deal and now the big ranch was ours!

But our *mamagrande* didn't want to move with us to our *rancho grande* in South Oceanside just a couple of miles north of *CarlosMalo*.

And of course, I didn't want to go without her, so I now also refused to move,

"*Mijito*," my grandmother said to me, "you need to go with your *familia*."

"But you are our *familia*, so come with us."

"Look at me," she said, stroking my face, "I'm old. My days are few. You're young. Your days are many."

"No, no! I don't want my days without you!"

"You'll never be without me," she said, smiling. "Remember the little bird's nest you didn't realize you saw until I had you close your HeadEyes and opened your HeartEyes?"

"Yes," I said.

"Well, *mijito*, every time you go to the bathroom in your new home, look up at those green vines and yellow flowers, and even with your HeadEyes you will now see that little bird nest."

"I will?"

"Yes, of course. And when the Hummingbirds return, you close your HeadEyes, open your HeartEyes, and you will see me."

"See you?" I asked, popping with excitement.

"Yes, with our HeartEyes we not only see all of Creation, we See the *Alma*Soul of Creation."

"We do?"

"Yes, that's why Our Loved Ones so often come to us as Hummingbirds and Butterflies from the Other Side of Living to visit with us on This side of Living.

"And when the hummingbird babies are born," she added, "you will SeeFeel them to be you and me. This is Our Ongoing Miracle of Life. For we are all Forever Birthing within Our Holy Breath of God."

"Then you and me will be these baby birds?" I asked, smiling with excitement.

"Exactly," she said. "Why do you think people get so happy and all excited when kittens are born? Or puppies are born?

"Why do you think that *Doña Cuca* loves her mother pig and little squealing baby pigs so much that she was willing to risk her life when she went after that truck driver with her broom?

"Why do you think Joseph and Mary ended up in a manger with a cow and a calf, and sheep and little lambs when *María* gave birth to Our Lord Jesus?

"You see, *mijito*, every newborn life reconnects us with Our Own Magic Adventure of us having come Birthing across Heaven along with Our Guardian Angel collecting StarDust.

"So *mijito*, you move with your *familia* to our *rancho grande*," she said, "for you have so much to learn from all the Birthing of horses and cattle and dogs, and especially from the ranch dog Shep, who was raised by his coyote mother.

"*Mundo*," she now said, making reference to my middle name, *Edmundo*, "and remember when you feel a little lost or scared, you close your HeadEyes and open your HeartEyes and you will feel the Purring of the Big Drum HeartBeat of Our Whole Entire Universe."

"Starting in my left ear," I said, smiling, "and going around the back of my head to my right ear."

"Exactly. And each generation brings their own Unique StarDust, and so each generation hears their own Unique Big DrumBeat which is the HeartPurring of –"

"– the HeartPurring of all Our Stars to the furthest reaches of our whole Universe," I added with excitement.

She laughed and her eyes danced with joy. "You've listened well, *mijito*. Come, let's hug."

I flew into her arms. Yes, oh, yes, I'd been young enough to listen and she'd gotten old enough to be a Sacred Elder.

And so now with this understanding of what to do if I ever felt a little lost or scared, I was able to move to our *rancho grande* in Oceanside along with my dad and mom and my older sister and brother.

And this was when I found out our mother was pregnant, and now also, because of all our parents' new American friends, including a hard drinking doctor, this child was going to be our *familia's* first baby born in a hospital.

Oh, things got so confusing!

And when we'd go to visit my *mamagrande* back in *CarlosMalo*, she'd looked so lonely and sick that she finally agreed to come live with us on the ranch.

Oh, I was so happy! BIG BIG HAPPY!

But she no longer got up early, so we could give Thanks to Our Father Sun along with Our Smiling Sister Flowers and Our Singing Brother Birds.

And I began feeling all cold, even when I got under the covers along with my *mamagrande*. It was like now that we weren't giving Thanks every morning to Our Father Sun, the Right Eye of God, I could no longer feel His warm cuddling good-feeling Purring.

Then as if this wasn't bad enough, our American doctor now told my mother our grandmother was sick, so I shouldn't sleep with her anymore.

I cried!

I screamed!

And my *mamagrande* told our mother she wanted to see our own healer, the *curandera*, who'd also been the midwife who'd brought me into the world.

The laughing colorfully-dressed old woman came and we were so happy to see her. Then after checking my grandmother, she told us that my *mamagrande* wasn't sick at all.

That she had just decided it was time for her to go, so it was fine for me to sleep with her.

Oh, this was wonderful!

And the Big DrumBeat of Our Universe instantly came back to me with warm good-feeling Purring.

And now once more I could cuddle with my *mamagrande* all day and night.

Then she Passed.

In her sleep, she Passed with a little quiet smile, and our old ranch and our old ranch house filled with guests, but I don't remember very much about any of this.

What I do remember very clearly is that a few nights after she'd Passed, she woke me up just before daybreak.

"Get up, my little Love*Amor*," she whispered to me, "and get dressed."

I glanced all around. I could hear her, but I couldn't see her.

"Just close your HeadEyes and open up your HeartEyes," she said.

I did as told, and instantly I saw her and she was smiling, and looking so young and beautiful.

"Put on your cowboy boots and meet me where I showed you the wild herbs grow down in the swampy area of our ranch."

I got dressed, then slipped on my little turquoise-colored boots, my Levi jacket, my cowboy hat, and hurried out our front door, running past our big fat happy laughing pepper tree.

From the hilltop, I could see that my *mamagrande* was with three other Native People just this side of the tall tulles.

I quickly went down the long hill. Sunlight was just starting to paint the sky behind me in colors of yellow and orange and pink, so it was still pretty dark and chilly down here in the swampy area.

"Come close," said my *mamagrande*. "These are some of the Original *Curanderos* of this Holy Garden of Healing Herbs. And they have gifted me the Great Honor of allowing me to join them.

"You see, *mijito*, we all come from our Mother Earth, so there's no earthly sickness that can't be healed with one of Her Herbs."

I could see that they each had a little knife with a hook in their right hand, the EarthWorking side of their body, and a small leather pouch on their left hip, the HeartGiving side of their body.

And their heads were bent down as they carefully searched among all the short green plants.

"*Mijito*, some of these little plants are Mother Moon Herbs, so these need to be cut before Our Father Sun touches them."

One slender old Native Healer came close, showing my grandmother the little plant he'd just cut.

Smiling, my *mamagrande* breathed a couple of gentle GodBreaths on the little plant, and instantly the little plant began to Glow.

The old Native Healer laughed, and he and my *mamagrande* both started quickly talking in their Native Tongue with such *gusto* that the whole Herb Garden began Purring with the Big DrumBeat of Our Universe.

Every plant.

Every group of plants.

Purring and Glowing and Chanting together in a Symphony of a soft gentle Whispering DrumBeat by the Sacred Eight Elders, who surrounded Our Big Drum, and were Passing HeartSoul Music to the next generation.

And then just like Magic, Our Father Sun began shooting beams of Golden Light overhead and across the tall tulles.

My grandmother and the three healers stopped their work, and they turned to face Our Miracle of another God-Gifted Day.

Smiling, my *mamagrande* took my hand, and I, too, now just couldn't stop smiling as we together faced the coming of Our Father Sun, the Right Eye of God, just as we'd done every morning back in our old *Barrio de CarlosMalo*.

And all was quiet.

Not a sound.

But then as the Golden Beams of Light came shooting across the land, giving Life, *la Vida* Magic to all of Creation Creating, the whole world suddenly EXPLODED with Sound!

First the frogs and then the crickets!

Hundreds of little frogs and big loud bullfrogs and millions of chirping crickets!

Then 1,000s of big Red Shouldered Blackbirds came singing and BURSTING out of the tulles!

And ducks, 100s of ducks, just beyond the tall tulles, began quacking loudly, and taking flight.

Laughing with excitement, I quickly turned to my grandmother, and she, too, was laughing with *carcajadas*.

Then right here in front of us, a doe and her little fawn now came out of the tulles, and they didn't shy away from us.

Oh, no, they came right up to us, and the little fawn reached out with her cute tiny nose to smell me, but she didn't try to smell my grandmother.

And the doe just stood there flicking her tail in peace, and in no hurry to get her fawn away from us.

I guess that we human people were just another natural part of nature.

Oh, I couldn't stop smiling, and I reached out to pet the fawn on her silky smooth-feeling pretty head, and along her long warm neck.

Oh, this was Heaven!

Right here! Right now! Forever and Ever!

Then out of the tulles here came a big mother skunk with five little baby skunks.

Oh, the tiny babies looked so cute and adorable, and two of the little skunks came right up to my turquoise-colored boots.

Smiling, I reached down and picked one up without any fear of being sprayed by their mother.

There was no Fear.

Fear can't exist when all is full to the brim with Trust and Love*Amor*.

The other baby skunk, who'd also come up to me, was now climbing up on the toe of my right boot, so I picked her up, too.

The doe and her fawn were now starting up the hillside behind me, leisurely grazing.

Then oh, Miracle of Miracles, before my very HeartEyes, the whole grassy green tall hillside now came ALIVE with 1,000s and 1,000s of little yellow flowers opening up and smiling with dancing joy to Our Right Eye of God!

And instantly, like right on cue, Song Birds began singing all about us, and it was now a Great Symphony of Music Giving Thanks to *Papito Dios* Our Holy Creator!

Then, as if this wasn't enough, now came the ear-piercing screaming SCREECH of our peacocks who roosted in the towering eucalyptus trees of the Magic Tunnel at the entrance of our *rancho grande*.

I turned to my *mamagrande* and she was all Aglow. And I didn't need to ask. I knew that I, too, was now all Aglow!

I put down the two little skunks and my grandmother and I now put our hands over our Heart*Corazones,* and we, too, began to sing along with all of Creation Creating, giving thanks to Our Father Sun, the Right Eye of God.

Tears of joy poured down my face. For now all day long I'd be seeing Life, *la Vida*, through Our Holy Creator's Right Eye, and I knew I'd always be part of Our Almighty's Heaven of Magic and Miracles.

"Well, *mijito*," my *mamagrande* now said to me, "it's time for me to now be going with my Fellow Spirit People, but I'll see you again *mañana*."

"You will?"

"Of course. Didn't I tell you that I'd never leave you, even long after I leave my earthly body and return to Spirit?"

"Yes, you did."

"*Mijito*, always remember that when a Loved One Passes, what they're really doing is bringing the whole Spirit World closer to you," she added, smiling and Aglowing even Brighter.

"Yes, with Hummingbirds and Butterflies!"

"Exactly."

"Oh, I love you so much!" I said, reaching out to hug her.

And she took me in her arms and we hugged, and kissed, and like always, she was all warm and plump, and so good-feeling.

Then after breathing in a few deep GodBreaths together, she gently pulled away from me and took my left ear in hand, adjusting it. Then my right ear and adjusting it.

And instantly I was really Purring!

Then she kissed me on my forehead, and looked at me Eye to Eye, *Alma*Soul to *Alma*Soul, and she was gone.

I smiled.

I laughed.

And my happy tears continued flowing.

For I now knew that my *mamagrande* who'd Passed and gone to Heaven was really Right Here with me Eye to Eye Forever – for this was Heaven. And she said she'd see me again tomorrow.

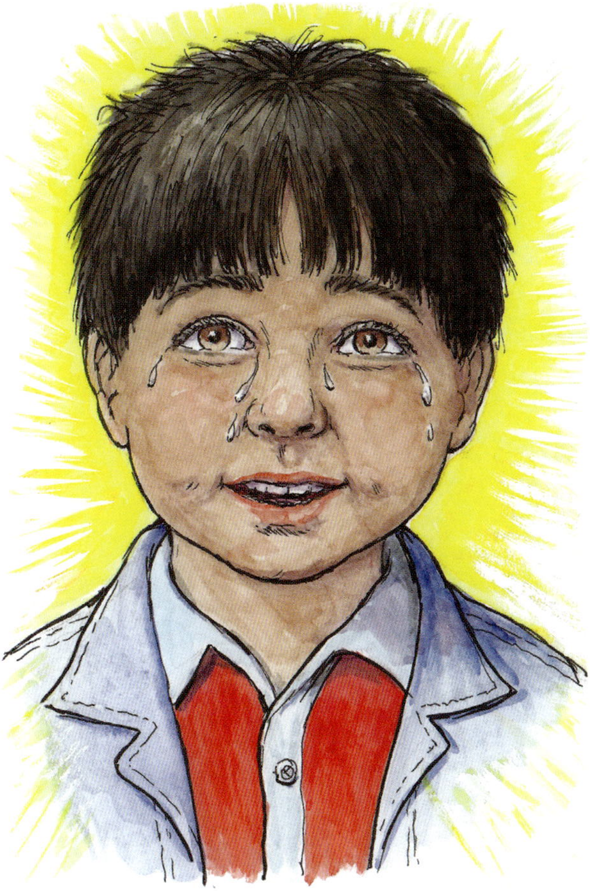

# NOW
# Who Are You?
# Who Am I?
# Who are We?

Well, I'd like you to know that a few months after my *mamagrande's* Passing, my baby sister Flora Linda was born.

And a few days after she was brought home from the hospital, I saw her looking past our parents and visiting relatives.

So I turned to see what she was looking at, and there was our grandmother all Aglow by the entrance of the door.

And this was wonderful. I was no longer alone seeing our *mamagrande*.

And recently, now that Linda and I are both in our Happy Joyful Blessed 80s, I asked my sister what were some of the first memories of her childhood.

"None," she said, "except one of a woman standing by the door. By herself. Apart from everyone else. And she was so full of Light that I felt, well, I guess safe and happy."

"And that's your only memory?"

"The only one that really stands out for me even to this day. She just stood there smiling and was so at peace and full of Light that like I said, I felt safe and happy."

So I now ask you, what are some of your first memories of your childhood?

Just take in a couple of big deep GodBreaths, and close your HeadEyes and open your HeartEyes, and you'll be surprised.

Magic Little Flashing Glimpses of GLOWING Light Memories will come to you, and you'll be so Happy! BIG BIG HAPPY!

HeartFelt
SoulGlowing

Little Flashing
Big Big Happy Memories

# Million Year Family

Men Our Heroes

Women Our Natural Leaders

Children Our Angels

One Race Our Human Race

# Gathering StarDust

You Me We

## About the Author

Victor Villaseñor, bestselling author of *Rain of Gold*, grew up in the *Barrio* of Carlsbad, California with his family and beloved *mamagrande*. He didn't speak English when he started school and flunked the third grade twice. He was in his 40s when he learned he is dyslexic off the charts auditorily and visually and that's why he didn't learn to read until he was in his 20s. The font used in *Gathering StarDust* is Lexie Readable, especially designed for dyslexic readers. Becoming a bestselling author proves that even those with disablities can achieve great things.

www.victorvillasenor.com
@victorvillasenor

## About the Illustrator

Jack lives in Ashland, Oregon where he spends time in nature and in his art studio. He has illustrated over 40 books, and written and illustrated *What Bear Said*, and *Tending Our Grief*. He was also a professional counselor for 33 years.

"There are no accidents. Jack Wiens was a Godsend and we are so thankful that this great illustrator who lives with a bear came to us and his bear joined hands with my *mamagrande* to guide him. We will be friends for life." —Victor

www.jackwiens.com

## DreamTeam StarDust

**This team of vibrant women were instrumental in creating this book. Dedicated to telling the story as Victor lived it, they each brought their own unique talents to the project.**

**Teri Rider** worked with Victor and Jack to make the story sing across the pages. Her delightful design of the book layout put it all together so you, the reader, can enjoy reading and sharing each page.

**Carmen Blum** is Victor's *Amor*, whom he marries anew each day in a beautiful little ritual. She is a Native *Mexicana*, from the State of Michoacán, and has been a San Diego North County Community Service Member for 35 years. Carmen offered her insights of culture, language, feelings and memories, embracing and connecting with the writing and illustrations of the Miraculous Spirituality that Gathering StarDust brings to all of humanity. Also, she did the final editing of the Spanish Translation.

**Linda Villaseñor**, Victor's intuitive sister, brought her real life memories to the stories as she recalled details of their *mamagrande* and family. Linda kept the messaging clear and engaging on social media about the upcoming book and all of the events surrounding its launch to then be successfully presented to the world.

**Gayle and Bill Gladstone,** the incomparable wife and husband team from Waterside Productions are long-time steadfast supporters of Victor's work. Gayle carried the torch after it was passed from her late husband, Bill, who so strongly believed in this little book, saying "Don't change a word!" insisting that it be one of the premier books he published before he left this earth. Gayle's mission is to help authors and filmmakers create a kinder, better world.

## Books by Victor Villaseñor

*Macho!*
*Jury: The People vs. Juan Corona*
*Rain of Gold*
*Snow Goose Global Thanksgiving*
*Wild Steps of Heaven*
*Thirteen Senses*
*Walking Stars*
*Burro Genius*
*Crazy Loco Love*
*Beyond Rain of Gold*
*Lion Eyes*
*Dolphin Miracles*
*Our First Woman Pope*

## Bilingual Children's Books:

*Frog and His Friends Save Humanity*
*The Stranger and the Red Rooster*
*Goodnight, Papito Dios*
*Little Crow to the Rescue*

## Screenplays:

*The Ballad of Gregorio Cortez*
*Walkout*